Uncle Andy's

BIBLE

STORIES

to say
and do!

to my sons...
Shelton
Andrew

Uncle Andy's Bible Stories to Say and Do

Copyright © 2000 Educational Publishing Concepts, Inc. Wheaton, IL

Published by New Kids Media™ in association with Baker Book House Company, Grand Rapids, Michigan.

ISBN 0-8010-4444-8

Printed in the United States of America

1 2 3 4 5 6 7 — 05 04 03 02 01 00

Uncle Andy's

BIBLE

STORIES

to say and do!

Written and Illustrated by Andy Holmes

published in
association with

My **THANKS** Page...

I especially wish to say thanks to Jerry Watkins, Jim Elwell and the folks at BAKER BOOKS for making this book series a reality. Not only that, I owe a thousand apologies (and thanks!) for everyone's extreme patience with me in completing these books. For your sakes, I hope for great success to make it all even more "worth it". The greatest of success will come with the first little child's interest, intrigue or affection for God's Word being established, prodded, or even, refreshed.

Thanks also to my best friend, Wendy! First, for marrying nearly 12 sweet years ago. Second, for blessing me with 3 precious babies. The oldest "baby" is 9, the middle "6", the last, AVY, only 1½ mo.!!! Thank you, Wendy, for all your work on these books.

Thanks also to Cassie (my sister-in-law) Ohlhausen for brainstorm'n and creating (along with Wendy) practically all of the activities. Thanks also to Sandy Noe for her thoughtful & creative contributions. Lastly, thanks to Gene Cordova for adding color to some of these pages.

— Andy

from Uncle Andy...

I hope you like these stories. The actual stories in the Bible are the greatest stories you'll ever read. I wrote this book to make you curious to read the real versions in a real Bible for yourself.

I had a lot of fun with some of these. Others caught me off-guard, made me think about them in fresh new ways. A few, especially the story of Jesus being crucified, made me sob like a man with a broken heart.

I hope these approaches I've taken will connect with you in ways that stay with you long after you close these covers.

Thanks for reading,
Uncle Andy

Little
Boy
Samuel

Samuel Hears God

(You can read this whole story in)
1 SAMUEL 3:1-21

Little boy Samuel
a'sleeping in his bed,
hears Somebody
   whisper,
and lifts
   his
 sleepy
  head.

He tiptoes beside Eli
and whispers, "I am here".
Eli yawns and shoo's him.
"Go back to bed, my dear".

As soon as he is sleeping, he hears his name once more.

He shuffles down to Eli's room as he had done before.

"Eli?", Samuel whispers,
"I heard you call my name".
Eli mumbles, "Child, it's
much too early for
these games."

Again Samuel's awakened
by the soothing voice.
Again, he visits Eli—
he feels he has no choice.

"I don't mean to disturb you, but I'm sure I heard you call

Eli sat up in his bed and thought about it all...

Then suddenly he smiled
and gave a knowing nod.

"My child," Eli
   told Samuel,

"The Voice you
    heard
  was God's."

Say & Do

Story: Samuel hears God

You will need: a pencil, paper (posterboard thickness
will work best), crayons (or markers), scissors

Draw cone-like
shape on paper:
Cut it
out→
Roll it
till sides
meet
↑
glue

Decorate megaphone with your own designs.

Act out the story with your family or friends.

Whoever plays God's part uses megaphone to call the
sleepy Samuel.

Have fun!

Give us a king!

King Saul

(You can read this whole story in
1 SAMUEL 8:1 – 10:25)

his displeased Samuel, so he prayed to God. "The people have not turned away from you, Samuel", God told him. "They have turned away from Me. Warn them about what a King will do to them".

King will take your daughters and make them cook for him", the old servant of God warned.

"A King will take your best animals for himself", Samuel told them. But the people wouldn't change their mind.

A tall man named Saul became their first king. Many kings followed. Some did what was right in God's sight. Many did not.

All that Samuel warned would happen, happened to them.

Say & Do

Story: Saul, Israel's first king

You'll need : crayons, one cardboard-type paper plate,
          Scissors, (glue & glitter, if desired)

Poke small hole in center of back of paper plate :   Draw "pizza slices"

Cut along each line.

Decorate with drawn "jewels" (or, glitter)

If you were God's chosen king, what types of laws would you make?

(For extra fun, ask permission to use a large towel or blanket for a robe)

Samuel learns a lesson

God looks at the Heart

(You can read this whole story in)
1 SAMUEL 16:1 – 13

"Fill your horn with oil, Samuel", God told h[
"and go to Jesse's house. I have chosen o[
new king. You must annoint him with oil".

But God said, "This is not the man I have chosen, Samuel. You're looking only at the outside, but I look at a man's heart".

Jesse brought seven sons to meet with Samuel. "The Lord has not chosen any of these.

Do you have another son?"

"Only my youngest," Jesse answered. "He's out in the fields tending the sheep."

"Send for him at once", Samuel told them. "I'll wait."

Say & Do

Story: God looks at the heart

You'll need: glitter, plastic confetti shapes, wiggle eyes, (especially hearts) small clear jar with tight-fitting lid, small non-dissolvable trinkets or toys, thick tacky white crafs glue, clear corn syrup

Fill the clear jar with corn syrup (not quite to top).

1. Put glitter, wiggle eyes, trinkets, plastic confetti, small toys (and whatever other small, non-dissolvable objects you'd like) into clear jar. (NOTE: Add a couple drops of water if corn syrup seems too "heavy" for confetti or glitter).

1.

2.

Glue all around top of the jar

3. Screw lid on. Let glue dry.

4. Shake it! Have fun!

God's 👁👁 look at our ♥s!

The bigger they are, the harder they fall!

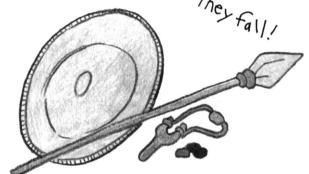

David and Goliath

(You can read this whole story in)
1 SAMUEL 17:1-54

Every morning and evening for forty days the Israelites listened to the mean Goliath's challenge. And each time they heard him, they shook with great fear.

Later, the shepherd boy David brings food from home to his brothers. He hears Goliath shouting.

"Who does this heathen Philistine think he is to mock the arm of the living God?" David asked.

"I will kill this Goliath!" David fumes.

"Go home, brat!," Eliab said. "You don't belong here!"

And king Saul said, "You're no match for Goliath. He is a strong warrior and you are a child."

And the Lord certainly did.

Say & Do

Story: David and Goliath

You'll need: an old sock or rag, smooth rocks (you find),
metal pan covered with foil, crayons

Find 5 smooth-surfaced stones.

Draw on stones with crayons.
(Simple drawings will do)

David Slingshot 5 stones Goliath God's Power

Place rocks on foil-covered pan. Cook 15 minutes
in oven at 200°. CAUTION: LET THEM COOL!

Polish rocks with old sock or rag to make them shine.

Using drawings on rocks as aides, tell someone
the story of David and Goliath.

Bring me a sword!

Wise King Solomon

(You can read this whole story in)
1 KINGS 3:16-28

There was a wise old kir
His name was Solomon
And when it came to 'smar
He was a brain phenomen

One time two ladies came
And stood before his throne
And fought about a baby
Now the story is well-known.

The first one screamed, "He's mine!
That woman stole my boy!
Her baby died late in the night
and now she wants my joy!"

The other woman screamed,
"She's lying to your face!
   Her baby died, and secretly,
   She put mine in his place!"

Then wise King Solomon
Said, "Tell ya what we'll do.
We'll take a sword and
cut this little baby into tw

e true mother cried out, "No, please! Give him to her!
ase don't harm my baby boy! Don't let this death occur!"

 other woman smiled a very evil smile, and said:
"Good thinking, King. Let us divide this little child."

"Aha!" the King announced,
"You've made it plain to see.
Give the child to this one
for she is his mommy."

Say & Do

Story: Wise King Solomon

You will need: paper, scissors, crayons (or markers)

Cut paper into "flash card" sized pieces.

Write one word on each card.

| Only | the | Lord | gives | Wisdom | Pr. 2:6 |

Help your child memorize this Bible verse. Then take one word out and see if your child can identify the "hidden" word.

Repeat this, taking a different word out each time.

Baal goes up in smoke

Elijah and the Prophets of Baal

(You can read this whole story in)
1 KINGS 18:16-46

.xcuse me, sir. Can you tell us what is about to happen here?

Elijah thinks his God JEHOVAH is better than our god Baal. He's challenged Baal to burn up an altar.

And will Baal do that?

Piece of cake.

"If Baal is really a god, call on him to start a f
and burn up this altar. Today the one true God
JEHOVAH will show you that Baal is only something m
up by men. An idol. Not a 'god' at all."

Well, the prophets of Baal have been crying out
Baal for hours and hours now but nothing (yawn)
I mean NOTHING - has happened. Nada. Zero. Zip.

can't believe it! Baal never showed up and
w Elijah has told the false prophets of Baal to
ood his altar with water! I believe in being
nfident but this is downright foolish! No one-
God or not- could start a
fire and burn up an altar
while it is drenched with
water! This is Crazy!

Say & Do

Story: Elijah and prophets of Baal

You will need: hand towel, scarf or pillow case, ribbon

Drape fabric (towel or pillow case) over head.

1.

2. Tie ribbon headband

3. Add scarf

You're Elijah! Read and pretend these cool stories about Elijah: 1 Kings 17:2-6; 1 Ki 17:7-24; 2 Ki. 2:11-12

It's a hot time in the ol' town tonight!

Shadrach, Meshach & Abednego

(You can read this whole story in)
DANIEL 3:1 – 30

Hi, boys and girls! I'm firefighter Faye and this is my amazing dog, Spartacus. What's so amazing about Spartacus? Well, Spartacus is not only a great fire dog and wonderful friend, he is also an incredible actor!

partacus and I want to tell you a story from
e Bible about 3 boys who got a lot closer to
fire than we hope you ever will. Actually, they
ent INSIDE a fire!

It started with a statue that was as tall as a building. It looked like King Nebuchadnezzar and was made of gold.

I said, Spartacus! So everybody bowed and began
rshipping this lifeless statue.

Everybody but
Shadrach, Meshach
and Abednego. They
said, "N–
oooooOoooOOOOOO!

Well said again, Spartacus! I see you have deci
to play co-narrator, too. King Nebuchadnezzar g
Shadrach, Meshach and Abednego one last chanc
"Boys," King Nebuchadnezzar warned them, "I v
throw you into this blazing hot fire if you do r

BOW-
WOW

Close, Spartacus. King "Nebby" didn't say, "Bow-Wow!", he said, "Bow!" And meant, "Bow *NOW!*" Still, the boys refused. "We will only bow down and worship the one true God!", they told the King. This made 'Nebby' so mad he threw the boys into the hot, hot, hot fire. (Spartacus is now playing the 3 boys in our story.)

"Now if you are ever in a fire - which we hope will never be - we'd tell you to STOP, DROP and ROLL. these boys had an even better source of protection: sent an angel to keep them safe in the fire. It was miracle! (Now Spartacus is playing the angel).

King Nebuchadnezzar was amazed!
"There's an angel of God in there with them!"
The King told the boys to come out and
shouted, "Praise be to the God of Shadrach,
Meshach and Abednego! Honor their God!"

And that's the end of this very, very true, um,

Tail!

Say & Do

Story: Shadrack, Meshach & Abednego

You will need: Crystal rose reynold's wrap, one old mitten, paper, crayons, double-sided tape, scissors

Draw and color 5 faces:
(* about the size of a quarter)
then cut them out.
Using double-sided tape,
attach a face to each finger
of mitten.

Shadrack · Meshach · Abednego
Angel   King

Do a puppet play!

Wow!
It looks like
Fire!

Tear 6" x 6" square
sheet a reynolds wrap.
Stick it to mirror
(by pressing only)

The fat cats meet the lions

Daniel

(You can read this whole story in)
DANIEL 6:1-28

Pardon me for whispering but I don't want that always-p Jew over there to hear my secret plan. Daniel prays to God even after I tricked King Darius into signing this clever idea of mine into a LAW. Teeheehee. I've done some bad things befor but this is my fines work by far.

ll, I suppose I can let the CAT out of the bag - if you
ch my drift. Speaking plainly, Daniel is as good as
ad! Teeheehee! How? Thanks to my smooth tongue, the
g made it against the law to say prayers to any god
man - except, of course, to King Darius. I knew that
niel would keep on praying to his God no matter what.

And best of all, if you break this law – as Dannyboy has – you will be thrown into the

LIONS' DEN!

"I am so sorry, my dear friend", I overheard a sad King Darius say. "I never thought this law would harm you."

Ha! What a foolish King! I tricked him big time!

Then King Darius nearly cried as he told Daniel, "I hope the God you serve so faithfully rescues you from these hungry lions".

What a softie this King Darius is!

Next thing I know, King Darius races in and shouts, "Daniel, has God saved you?" And Daniel answers, "Yes!" He pulls Daniel out and throws me and all the others who tricked the King into signing this law into the **Lions' den!**

Say & Do

Story: Daniel in lion's den

You will need: 'face and body'washable paint (yellow, lt. brown),
1 black pipe cleaner, two wiggles (or you can
make paper eyes), 1 paper baking cup, glue (or,
double-sided tape), 8" piece of brown yarn

Start in middle of pipe cleaner. Wrap it
around end of middle finger. Twist it to
hold its place. Make 2 more loops
for eyes. Glue eyes
to loops

Flatten paper baking cup. Cut hole for finger.
Tie yarn loosely around wrist with extra length for tail.
Paint hand tan, yellow or light brown. Paint lion's nose
and mouth. Assemble on hand as shown above.

Hook, Line and Sinker

Jonah

(You can read this whole story in JONAH 1:1–4:11)

"Tell me again, Grandpa! Tell me again!" Little Fish squeaked. "Tell me about the time you swallowed that squirmy, long thing!"

"Well, all right," Grandpa agreed. "It was a dark, dark night. The waters were splashing and twirling and spinning."

"Yes, Little Fish," Grandpa said. "The roughest storm I've ever seen."

And it started choking you, right, Grandpa? nd it made you so sick in your tummy that you threw up, right, Grandpa?! Right?! Right?!!
"Not exactly," said Grandpa. "I felt fine for a few days."
Yeah, but THEN it made you throw up! Right, Grandpa?!

"The strange, squirmy thing I swallowed was a m[an]
named Jonah," Grandpa explained. "Jonah was run[ning]
from God. God used me to help change Jonah's attit[ude]

fter 3 days, Jonah was ready to obey God."
And THEN you threw up! Right, Grandpa?!!!
"I guess you could put it that way. I spit Jonah out."
Cool!!

"Once Jonah was back on dry land, he obeyed God's call to to Nineveh and tell the people to turn to God. The, er, 'Coo thing is that the people of Nineveh listened to Jonah a asked God to forgive them for their evil ways. And course, God did, a Nineveh was save

Do you have any questions, Little Fish?"
Yes, Grandpa. Are there any more stories where you throw up?!!
"Thankfully, no."

Say & Do

Story: Jonah

You will need: 1 small party balloon, one small dried
bean (pinto, lima), marker (to draw on balloon)

Insert dried bean into uninflated balloon.

Inflate balloon.

Draw fish face, gills and fins on balloon.

Shake fish balloon and you'll
hear "Jonah" bouncing around in fish's tummy!